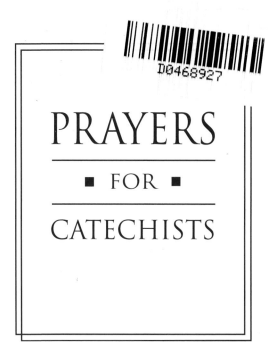

PRAYERS

■ FOR ■

CATECHISTS

LITURGY
TRAINING
PUBLICATIONS

ACKNOWLEDGMENTS

This book was compiled by Jeanette Lucinio, SP, with the assistance of her class, "Holistic Parish Religious Education" at Catholic Theological Union in Chicago in the spring of 2000.

The book was edited by Lorie Simmons with assistance from Gabe Huck, Margaret Brennan and Lorraine Schmidt. Audrey Novak Riley was the production editor. The design is by Anne Fritzinger, who typeset it in Galliard. The cover image is by Don Bishop © 1997 Artville, LLC. The interior art is by Ronda Krum. Printed by Printing Arts Chicago.

Texts were contributed by Michel Andreos, Mary Ann Bernot, Chuck Gamen, Stephane Kalonji, Loc Quang Tran and Vivian E. Williams.

We are grateful to the many publishers and authors who have given permission to include their work. Every effort has been made to determine the ownership of all texts and to make proper arrangements for their use. We will gladly correct in future editions any oversight or error that is brought to our attention.

Unless otherwise noted, excerpts from scripture are from the *New Revised Standard Version of the Bible* © 1989 Division of Christian Education of the National Council of the Churches of Christ in the United States of America. All rights reserved.

Excerpts of the Psalms are from *The Psalms: Grail Translation from the Hebrew* © 1993 by Ladies of the Grail (England). Used by permission of GIA Publications, Inc., exclusive agent. All rights reserved.

Acknowledgments continued on page 59.

FOREWORD

*How beautiful are the feet of those
who bring the good news!*
Jesus prayed that God would call workers into
the vineyard—and you have answered. As a
catechist you will have many desires and
experiences that cry out for prayer and ponder-
ing. This little book has been prepared for you,
no matter what the circumstances of your
ministry—whether you work with children or
adults, in meeting rooms, homes, or classrooms.
Use it in your daily prayer; turn to it before or
after you have prepared your sessions. Let the
insights of these prayers and reflections seep in
gradually as you return to them often.

Each catechist prays out of a different set
of ever-shifting circumstances and so have the
many contributors to this book, many long
departed. Some point us toward the delicate
movements of the Spirit; others exhort us to
steelier positions—courage in the face of
poverty and violence. All of these perspectives

are poignant catalysts for prayer, and show us vividly the many ways that catechists serve and pray in order to bring about the kingdom.

Prayers need not always rise like incense; they may roil around in our minds as ruminations. In catechesis we are often breaking open the word; in prayer we are prying open the heart, hoping to break through to a fresh awareness of God's nearness. These prayers and reflections should create some cracks.

Catechesis is a ministry of the word and the Word you echo is Jesus, the Word made flesh. As catechists, you lead others to Christ and his teaching—realities you once received from catechists and continue to deepen in your own discipleship. May these prayers and reflections feed your spirituality, out of which all good catechesis flows. May you be found faithful to your calling.

—*Jeanette Lucinio,* SP

Called with a Holy Calling

Do not be ashamed, then, of the testimony about our Lord or of me, his prisoner, but join with me in suffering for the gospel, relying on the power of God, who saved us and called us with a holy calling.

—*2 Timothy 1:8–9*

Entrusted with the Word

Now the word of the LORD came to me saying,
"Before I formed you in the womb I knew you,
and before you were born I consecrated you;
I appointed you a prophet to the nations."
Then I said, "Ah, Lord GOD! Behold, I do not
know how to speak, for I am only a youth."

But the LORD said to me,
"Do not say, 'I am only a youth';
for to all to whom I send you you shall go
and whatever I command you you shall speak.
Be not afraid of them,
    for I am with you to deliver you."

Then the LORD put forth his hand and
touched my mouth; and the LORD said to me,
"Behold, I have put my words in your mouth."

   —Jeremiah 1:4–9 RSV

O God of infinite glory,
to our unclean lips and faltering hands
you entrust the responsibility
of bearing to all the proclamation of the gospel.

Sustain us with your Spirit,
that through our witness
your word may find an eager welcome
in every heart
and bear a rich harvest
in every corner of the world.

We ask this through Christ our Lord. Amen.

—*Peter J. Scagnelli*

For "Everyone who calls on the name of the Lord will be saved." But how are they to call on one in whom they have not believed? And how are they to believe in one of whom they have never heard? And how are they to hear without someone to proclaim him? And how are they to proclaim him unless they are sent? As it is written, "How beautiful are the feet of those who bring good news!"

—*Romans 10:13–15*

Sent to Share

God our Father,
in your goodness and concern for the world,
you anoint and consecrate messengers
who are sent to share your life and love.
Jesus is *the* prophet;
we are called
to put on his mind and heart
and to share in his anointing.
May your Spirit be upon us.
Grant this through your Son,
our Lord Jesus. Amen.

> —*Robert F. Morneau*

Thanks be to God, who in Christ always leads
us in triumphal procession, and through us
spreads in every place the fragrance that comes
from knowing him. For we are not peddlers of
God's word like so many; but in Christ we
speak as persons of sincerity, as persons sent
from God.

> —*2 Corinthians 2:14, 17*

Full and Robust Proclamation

Catechesis is an echoing of the gospel. It is a ministry of the word that proclaims the good word of God in Jesus. It is a full and robust proclamation that invites the full person to a response in faith, a response embodied in charity and justice.

—*Thomas H. Morris*

The things we have heard and understood,
the things our ancestors have told us,
these we will not hide from their children
but will tell them to the next generation:
the glories and might of the LORD
and the marvelous deeds God has done,
setting a witness in Jacob,
and establishing the law in Israel.

—*Psalm 78:3–5*

Yours is a share
in the work of the Lord's Spirit
who calls women, men and children
to faith and to communion with the church,
the assembly of believers, the body of Christ.
Yours is the task of echoing
the voice of God, who speaks and calls with love
in the hearts and minds
of inquirers, catechumens and the elect. . . .
Come to your work
from your personal prayer,
the wellspring from which your faith is refreshed.
Come to your ministry
with your heart open to all the ways
the Lord may move, shape, mold and form you
as an icon of his presence for the catechumens.
Immerse yourself in the scriptures
of the Lord's story
so that his story becomes yours
and you become his . . . .
Be faithful in the work you do,
for through it the Lord saves his people.

—*Austin Fleming*

The catechists became the spokespersons for the community's reflection and not like teachers who offer a reflection already prefabricated. The word of God was being reflected upon in the heart of the communities, taking their own lived situations as the point of departure; the catechists were "the harvesters of the fruit of the community's reflection." Without the selfless dedication of our servants of the word and of the catechists, the advances in evangelization would be very few. The catechists have called together the communities at least once a week and have nourished the faith of the communities with their words, their examples and their actions.

—*Samuel Ruiz Garcia*

What Do You Want from Me?

I am yours and for you I was born:
what do you want from me?

I am yours because you created me,
yours because you redeemed me,
yours because you bore with me,
yours because you called me to you,
yours because you also waited for me
and did not have me condemned.
What do you want from me?

In your love, then, give me wisdom,
or give me ignorance;
let me have years of plenty
or years of leanness and hunger;
let me be in darkness
or in the bright light of day;
send me wherever you wish.
What do you want from me?

—*Teresa of Avila, sixteenth century*

O Lord Jesus Christ,
you have laid your hand on us,
You called us by name,
you have commanded us:
"Go, teach all nations."
We ask you: Put your love into our hearts.
Put your understanding into our minds,
put your words into our mouths.
May we always raise and serve you,
who live and reign with the Father
and the Holy Spirit,
one God forever and ever. Amen.

—Nigerian Catechists' Prayer

Prepare the Way for the People

Go through, go through the gates,
prepare the way for the people;
build up, build up the highway,
clear it of stones.

—*Isaiah 62:10*

We Call upon You

Since Christ has called, let him be called upon.
Say to him: You have called us; we call upon
you. We have understood your vocation; hear
our invocation. Bring us to where you have
promised. Perfect what you have begun. Do
not abandon your own gifts; do not abandon
your own field. Let your plants enter your barn!

—*Augustine of Hippo, fourth century*

With the cord of your charity
you have bound us,
and in your light
you have given us light.
So if we open the eye of our understanding
with a will to know you,
we know you,
for your light enters into every soul
who opens the gate of her will.
For the light stands at the soul's gate,
and as soon as the gate is opened to it,
the light enters.

You, light, make the heart simple,
not two-faced.
You make it big,
not stingy—
so big that it has room in its loving charity
for everyone: with well-ordered charity
it seeks everyone's salvation.

—*Catherine of Siena, fourteenth century*

O Wisdom

Wisdom teaches her children
and gives help to those who seek her.
Whoever loves her loves life,
and those who seek her from early morning
    are filled with joy.
Whoever holds her fast inherits glory,
and the Lord blesses the place she enters.
Those who serve her minister to the Holy One;
the Lord loves those who love her.

—*Sirach 4:11–14*

But as for you, continue in what you have learned and firmly believed, knowing from whom you learned it, and how from childhood you have known the sacred writings that are able to instruct you for salvation through faith in Christ Jesus. All scripture is inspired by God and is useful for teaching, for reproof, for correction, and for training in righteousness, so that everyone who belongs to God may be proficient, equipped for every good work.

—*2 Timothy 3:14–17*

Hear our prayers, Lord Jesus,
the everlasting Wisdom of God the Father.
You give us, in our youth, aptness to learn.
Add, we pray, the furtherance of your grace,
so to learn knowledge and the liberal sciences
that, by their help, we may attain
to a fuller knowledge of you,
whom to know is the height of blessedness.

—*Erasmus, fifteenth century*

Deeply Serious and without Trappings

The adult has lost in relationship with God the essentiality that is one of the most characteristic aspects of the religious personality of the child. The younger the child the more capable of receiving great things, and the child is satisfied only with the great and essential things. The child's interior life is deeply serious and without trappings.

—*Sofia Cavalletti*

"Please, Lamb," said Lucy, "is this the way to Aslan's country?"

"Not for you," said the Lamb. "For you the door into Aslan's country is from your own world."

"What!" said Edmund. "Is there a way into Aslan's country from our world too?"

"There is a way into my country from all worlds," said the Lamb; but as he spoke his snowy white flushed tawny gold and his size changed and he was Aslan himself, towering above them and scattering light from his mane.

"O Aslan," said Lucy. "Will you tell us how to get into your country from our world?"

"I shall be telling you all the time," said Aslan. . . . "And now come; I will open the door in the sky and send you to your own land."

"Please, Aslan," said Lucy. "Before we go will you tell us when we can come back to Narnia again?" . . .

"Dearest," said Aslan very gently, "you and your brother will never come back to Narnia."

"Oh, *Aslan!!*" said Edmund and Lucy both together in despairing voices. . . .

"It isn't Narnia, you know," sobbed Lucy. "it's *you*. We shan't meet *you* there. And how can we live, never meeting you?"

"But you shall meet me, dear one," said Aslan.

"Are—are you there too, Sir?" said Edmund.

"I am," said Aslan. "But there I have another name. You must learn to know me by that name. This was the reason you were brought to Narnia, that by knowing me here for a little, you may know me better there."

—*C. S. Lewis*

Listening

Listening is a skill that grows dull in the barrage of words one hears all day long. Yet we have no substitute for it. In the liturgy we are schooled in the art of listening. What we do here, we are to do with our lives—be good listeners to one another, to the Lord, to the world with all its needs. This kind of listening is not passive—it is something *we do*. It is listening with the whole self, mind and heart and soul.

—*Joseph Bernardin*

Listening in community is always enriching. Listening with children is especially so, in our estimation, because God's word resounds in a different manner in young children than in adults, and thus it is through children that another nuance of the word reaches us.

This openness to listening is a fundamental educative element for children and adults. Listening is the leaning toward others, the opening of ourselves in a receptive attitude toward the reality around us; it is only the capacity to listen that prevents us from revolving around ourselves.

—*Sofia Cavalletti*

Lord Jesus Christ,
open the ears and eyes of my heart,
that I may hear and understand your Word
and do your will.
I am a pilgrim on earth;
hide not your commandments from me.
Take away the covering from my eyes,
that I may see wonderful things in your law.

—*Ephrem of Syria, fourth century*

Lord Jesus,
merciful and patient,
grant us grace, we beseech Thee,
ever to teach in a teachable spirit;
learning along with those we teach,
and learning from them
whenever Thou so pleasest;
that we and they may all be taught of God.

—*Christina Rossetti, nineteenth century*

Speak through Me

Lord, you have given us a tongue
to sing and shout your praise.
But you have made reality
so much greater than our minds and our lips.
Grace us to embrace your mystery
and to speak as adequately as we can
the mysteries of your love and forgiveness.
May Jesus, the risen Lord,
utter words that we cannot speak on our own.
May glory be yours forever. Amen.

—*Robert F. Morneau*

Moses said to the LORD, "O my Lord, I have never been eloquent, neither in the past nor even now that you have spoken to your servant; but I am slow of speech and slow of tongue." Then the LORD said to him, "Who gives speech to mortals? Is it not I, the LORD? Now go, and I will be with your mouth and teach you what you are to speak."

—*Exodus 4:10–12*

For the Holy Spirit will teach you at that very hour what you ought to say.

—*Luke 12:12*

Lord Jesus,
teach me, that I may teach them;
sanctify and enable all my powers,
that in their full strength
I may deliver thy message reverently,
readily, faithfully, and fruitfully.
Make thy word a swift word,
passing from the ear to the heart,
from the heart to life and conversation;
that as the rain returns not empty,
so neither may thy word,
but accomplish that for which it is given.
O Lord, hear;
O Lord, forgive;
O Lord, hearken;
and do so for thy blessed Son's sake.

—*George Herbert, seventeenth century*

Strengthen Our Souls

Blessed Lord,
by whose providence
all holy scriptures were written
and preserved for our instruction,
give us grace to study them
this and every day with patience and love.
Strengthen our souls
with the fullness of their divine teaching.
Keep from us all pride and irreverence.
Guide us in the deep things
of thy heavenly wisdom,
and of thy great mercy lead us by thy word
unto everlasting life;
through Jesus Christ our Lord and Savior.
Amen.

—*Brooke Foss Westcott, nineteenth century*

We begin by re-animating our faith in the power the word possesses to reach out to us wherever we are, and to provide the direction and zest we need to intensify our journey toward God.

—*Michael Casey*

Blessed are you, O LORD;
    teach me your statutes.
LORD, let your love come upon me,
    the saving help of your promise.
And I shall answer those who taunt me
    for I trust in your word.
Do not take the word of truth from my mouth
    for I trust in your decrees.
I will speak of your will before the powerful
    and not be abashed.
Your commands have been my delight;
    these I have loved.
Teach me discernment and knowledge
    for I trust in your commands.

—*Psalm 119:12, 41–44, 46–47, 66*

Let us not tire of preaching love,
it is the force that will overcome the world.
Let us not tire of preaching love.
Though we see that waves of violence
succeed in drowning the fire of Christian love,
love must win out, it is the only thing that can.

—*Oscar Romero*

Give me strength today,
O Lord God of Israel!

—*Judith 13:7*

Examine Yourselves

Examine yourselves to see whether you are living in the faith. Test yourselves. Do you not realize that Jesus Christ is in you?

—2 Corinthians 13:5

In the Counsel of Your Heart

Heed the counsel of your own heart,
for no one is more faithful to you than it is.
For our own mind sometimes
    keeps us better informed
than seven sentinels sitting high
    on a watchtower.

    —Sirach 37:13–14

Above all pray to the Most High
    to guide you on the way of truth.

    —Sirach 37:15, REB

O Lord, our God!
We bring now before thee all that troubles us:
our failings, errors, and exaggerations,
    our tribulations, our sorrows,
and also our rebelliousness
    and bitterness—
our whole heart, our whole life,
which thou knowest better than we ourselves.
We place it all in the faithful hands
which thou hast stretched out to us
    in our Savior.
Take us as we are;
raise up those who are weak,
enrich from thy fullness those who are poor.
Give clarity and courage
to those who proclaim thy word!

—*Karl Barth*

Dear Lord,
Not a good day. I lost my grip!
Lesson out of focus and unfinished.
Yet the children seemed happy when they left.
They must have felt you—
in spite of my confusions.
Help me to accept this day
and to trust that you will focus and guide me
at our next meeting.
Your will, not mine,
leads us to share our stories of you.

—Rosa A. Rivera-Mizzoni

With a Humbled Spirit

O Son of David,
I approach you with a humbled spirit.
In the hope and strength
    that you have given me,
I dare to speak to you.
With the key of your cross
open up the secrets of my heart;
send one of the seraphim
with a burning coal from your altar
to cleanse my soiled lips.
Grant that my tongue,
in loving service of my neighbor,
may never speak in error but bravely
and without ceasing proclaim your truth.

—*Julian of Toledo, seventh century*

Give judgement for me, O LORD,
for I walk the path of perfection.
I trust in the LORD; I have not wavered.
Examine me, LORD, and try me;
O test my heart and my mind,
for your love is before my eyes
and I walk according to your truth.

—*Psalm 26:1–3*

My Lord God,
I have no idea where I am going.
I do not see the road ahead of me.
I cannot know for certain where it will end.
Nor do I really know myself,
and the fact that I think I am following
    your will
does not mean that I am actually doing so.
But I believe that the desire to please you
does in fact please you.
And I hope I have that desire
in all that I am doing.

I hope that I will never do anything
apart from that desire.
And I know that if I do this
you will lead me by the right road,
though I may know nothing about it.
Therefore I will trust you always
though I may seem to be lost
and in the shadow of death.
I will not fear, for you are ever with me,
and you will never leave me
to face my perils alone.

—*Thomas Merton*

The Sower's Yield

Jesus said, "Listen! A sower went out to sow. And as he sowed, some seed fell on the path, and the birds came and ate it up. Other seed fell on rocky ground, where it did not have much soil, and it sprang up quickly, since it had no depth of soil. And when the sun rose, it was scorched; and since it had no root, it withered away. Other seed fell among thorns, and the thorns grew up and choked it, and it yielded no grain. Other seed fell into good soil and brought forth grain, growing up and increasing and yielding thirty and sixty and a hundredfold." And he said, "Let anyone with ears to hear listen!"

—*Mark 4:3–9*

Like scattered seed,
whose growth is slow but steady,
your kingdom is revealed, O God.
At first so small,
its harvest provides for all who hunger.

Turn to us who measure progress
by standards so different from your own.
Give us trust in your ways of planting,
patience with gentle nurturing,
until we come to rest
in the great branches of the cross.
We ask this through Christ our Lord. Amen.

—*Peter J. Scagnelli*

It helps now and then to step back
and take the long view.
The kingdom is not only beyond our efforts;
it is even beyond our vision.
We accomplish in our lifetime only
    a tiny fraction
of the magnificent enterprise that is
    God's work. . . .
Nothing we do is complete,
which is another way of saying
that the kingdom always lies beyond us.
No statement says all that could be said.
No prayer fully expresses our faith.
No confession brings perfection,
no pastoral visit brings wholeness.
No program accomplishes the church's mission.
No set of goals and objectives
    includes everything.
This is what we are about:
We plant the seeds that one day will grow.
We water seeds already planted,
knowing that they
hold future promise. . . .

We lay foundations that will need
    further development.
We provide yeast that produces effects
far beyond our capabilities.
We cannot do everything,
and there is a sense of liberation
    in realizing that.
This enables us to do something
and to do it very well.
It may be incomplete, but it is a beginning,
a step along the way, an opportunity
for God's grace to enter and do the rest.
We may never see the end results,
but that is the difference
between the master builder and the worker.
We are workers, not master builders—
ministers, not messiahs.
We are prophets of a future not our own.

—*Oscar Romero*

Grant Us Grace

Grant us, we beseech thee, O Lord,
grace to follow thee whithersoever thou goest.
In little daily duties to which thou callest us,
bow down our wills to simple obedience,
patience under pain or provocation,
strict truthfulness or word or manner,
humility and kindness.
In great acts of duty or perfection,
if thou shouldst call us to them,
uplift us to sacrifice and heroic courage;
that in all things, both small and great,
we may be imitators of thy dear Son,
even Jesus Christ our Lord.

—Christina Rossetti, nineteenth century

Lord, temper with tranquillity
our manifold activity
that we may do our work for thee
with very great simplicity.

—Anonymous, sixteenth century

Teach me to profit
by the suffering that comes across my path.
Let me so use it that it may mellow me,
not harden nor embitter me,
that it may make me patient,
not irritable,
that it may make me broad in my forgiveness,
not narrow, haughty, nor overbearing.
May my life be lived in the supernatural,
full of power for good,
and strong in its purpose of holiness.

—*John Henry Newman, nineteenth century*

My Lord!
We can do nothing without your help.
In the name of your divine compassion
do not let this soul be misled,
or turn aside from the path it has taken.
Give it your light,
to see that its well-being
depends on continuing along that path.

—*Teresa of Avila, sixteenth century*

Let not thy Word, O Lord,
become a judgment upon us,
that we hear it and do it not,
that we know it and love it not,
that we believe it and obey it not:
O thou, who with the Father
and the Holy Spirit
livest and reignest, world without end. Amen.

—*Thomas à Kempis, fifteenth century*

You show us
that your compassion will avail us not at all
unless we ourselves are compassionate.
And from this it is clear
that, though you created us without our help,
you do not want to save us without our help.
You want us,
merciful and compassionate Father,
to look at your boundless compassion for us,
so that we may learn to be compassionate,
first of all to ourselves
and then to our neighbors—
So you want the soul to look
at your compassion
so that she may rise above her own cruelty
and accept the food your compassion offers
to nourish her and give her life.

—*Catherine of Siena, fourteenth century*

Be present, most merciful God, and protect us
through the silent hours of this night,
so that we who are wearied
by the changes and chances of this world,
may take rest in your abiding changelessness.
Through Christ our Lord. Amen.

—*Ambrose, fourth century*

Draw Water from the Wells of Salvation

With joy you will draw water
from the wells of salvation.

—*Isaiah 12:3*

Source of Life

Jesus came to a Samaritan city called Sychar, near the plot of ground that Jacob had given to his son Joseph. Jacob's well was there, and Jesus, tired out by his journey, was sitting by the well. It was about noon. A Samaritan woman came to draw water, and Jesus said to her, "Give me a drink." (His disciples had gone to the city to buy food.) The Samaritan woman said to him, "How is it that you, a Jew, ask a drink of me, a woman of Samaria?" (Jews do not share things in common with Samaritans.) Jesus answered her, "If you knew the gift of God, and who it is that is saying to you, 'Give me a drink,' you would have asked him, and he would have given you living water." The woman said to him, "Sir, you have no bucket, and the well is deep. Where do you get that living water? Are you greater than our ancestor Jacob, who gave us the well, and with his sons and his flocks drank from it?" Jesus said to her, "Everyone who drinks of this water will be thirsty again, but those who drink of the water that I will give them will never be thirsty. The water that I will give will become in them a spring of water gushing up to eternal life." The woman said to him, "Sir, give me this water, so that I may never be thirsty or have to keep coming here to draw water."

—*John 4:5–15*

Let us leave a little room for reflection, room too for silence. Enter into yourself, and leave behind all noise and confusion. Look within yourself.

See whether there be some delightful hidden place in your consciousness where you can be free of noise and argument, where you need not be carrying on your disputes and planning to have your own stubborn way. Hear the word in quietness, that you may understand it.

—*Augustine of Hippo, fourth century*

Lord,
keep us still
as time turns on its hinges
like a creaky door.
We cannot go on forever
lifting the ram's horn
to blow our screeching questions.
Hold us in soundlessness
with mind polished
a brass mirror in which faintly at first
a reflection appears
an imprint intensified
from moment to moment
from year to year.

—*Catherine de Vinck*

The Word of God Is Living and Active

Brothers and sisters, here is a question for you: Which to you seems the greater, the word of God or the body of Christ? If you want to give the right answer, you will reply that God's word is not less than Christ's body. Therefore, just as we take care when we receive the body of Christ that no part of it falls to the ground, so should we likewise ensure that the word of God which is given to us is not lost to our souls because we are speaking or thinking about something different. One who listens negligently to God's word is just as guilty as one who, through carelessness, allows Christ's body to fall to the ground.

—*Caesarius of Arles, fifth century*

For the great Fathers, inspiration is not just something that acted once on the sacred writers, resulting in the inspired texts. It is an ongoing and ever-present influence at work within the books themselves, which are and remain inspired. The presence of the Spirit who once dictated the scriptures insures their perennial youth (to borrow a phrase from Irenaeus) and continues to breathe life into them. They remain filled with the Spirit of God.

—*Mariano Magrassi*

Indeed, the word of God is living and active, sharper than any two-edged sword, piercing until it divides soul from spirit, joints from marrow; it is able to judge the thoughts and intentions of the heart.

—*Hebrews 4:12*

Meditation Is like a Cherishing

Let us keep the scriptures in mind and meditate upon them day and night, persevering in prayer, always on the watch. Let us beg the Lord to give us real knowledge of what we read and to show us not only how to understand it but how to put it into practice, so that we may deserve to obtain spiritual grace, enlightened by the law of the Holy Spirit, through Jesus Christ our Lord, whose power and glory will endure throughout the ages.

—*Origen, third century*

In the Middle Ages, the word *meditatio* was not restricted to mental activity. It was viewed instead as musing, an almost audible process of repeating texts to oneself, a rumination. It was certainly not a high-powered operation, like a quick raid into a text to grab the meaning and make an escape. More like a friendship, a cherishing, whereby one lived with a text that had become particularly dear, exploring it from different vantage points, saying it to oneself in a quiet, non-analytic way and letting it act on the heart. This process reached throughout the day and into every corner of life. Its beginning was in the practice of holy reading.

—*Michael Casey*

O Lord,
you have given us your word for a light
to shine upon our path;
grant us so to meditate on that word,
and to follow its teaching,
that we may find in it the light that shines
more and more until the perfect day;
through Jesus Christ our Lord.

—*Jerome, fourth century*

Oh Book! infinite sweetness! let my heart
Suck every letter, and a honey gain.

—*George Herbert*

Happy is the person who meditates on wisdom.

—*Sirach 14:20*

Barriers and Breakthroughs

How is it that, when there is so little time
to enjoy your presence, you hide from me?

—*Teresa of Avila, sixteenth century*

There is a really deep well inside me. And in it
dwells God. Sometimes I am there too. But
more often stones and grit block the well, and
God is buried beneath. Then God must be dug
out again.

—*Etty Hillesum*

Late have I loved you,
Beauty so ancient and so new,
late have I loved you!
Lo, you were within,
but I outside, seeking there for you,
and upon the shapely things you have made
I rushed headlong, I, misshapen.
You were with me, but I was not with you.
They held me back far from you,
those things which would have no being
were they not in you.
You called, shouted,
broke through my deafness;
you flared, blazed, banished my blindness;
you lavished your fragrance, I gasped,
and now I pant for you;
I tasted you, and I hunger and thirst;
you touched me, and I burned for your peace.

—*Augustine of Hippo, fourth century*

Flood My Soul

Lord,
help me to spread your fragrance everywhere.
Flood my soul with your Spirit and life;
penetrate and possess my whole being
so completely that my life
may only be a radiance of yours.
Shine through me, and be so in me that
every soul with whom I come in contact
may feel your presence within my soul.
Let them look up and no longer see me,
but only you, Jesus.

—*John Henry Newman, nineteenth century*

You wait for us
until we are open to you.
We wait for your word
to make us receptive.
Attune us to your voice,
to your silence,
speak and bring your Son to us—
Jesus, the word of your peace.
Your word is near,
O Lord our God,
your grace is near.
Come to us, then,
with mildness and power.
Do not let us be deaf to you,
but make us receptive and open
to Jesus Christ your Son,
who will come to look for us and save us
today and every day for ever and ever. Amen.

—*Huub Oosterhuis*

Somewhere
beyond the boundaries
of body, house, street
a space opens
place of pilgrimage
to which I ascend
not on hands and knees
not crawling through mental routes
but
flying
with heavy flesh made light
with arms invisibly feathered
spread like great supportive wings.

A time of arrival, of exploration
of becoming part of the eternal hosannah.

—*Catherine de Vinck*

Acknowledgments continued

Now the word, p. 2: *Revised Standard Version of the Bible* © 1952, Division of Christian Education of the National Council of Churches of Christ in the United States of America. All rights reserved.

O God, p. 3; Like scattered, p. 35: *Prayers for Sundays and Seasons,* Liturgy Training Publications (LTP), Chicago.

God our Father, p. 5; Lord, you, p. 21: *Mantras for the Morning; Mantras for the Evening,* Liturgical Press, Collegeville. Used by permission of Robert Morneau.

Catechesis is, p. 6: *The RCIA: Transforming the Church,* © 1989 Thomas H. Morris: Paulist Press, Mahwah, New Jersey.

Yours is, p. 7: *Preparing for Liturgy,* LTP.

The catechists, p. 8: "Ministry of the Church in Chiapas," *Origins,* vol. 23, no. 34.

I am, p. 9; My Lord, p. 40: *Praying with Saint Teresa,* compiled by Battistina Capalbo, tr. Paula Clifford. Wm. B. Eerdsman Publishing Co., Grand Rapids, Michigan, 1997.

O Lord, p. 10: *Training for Catechetics Programme* for the Seventh Nigerian National Catechetical Week, October 1998. Produced by the National Association of Directors of Religious education, Ede, Osun State, Nigeria.

Since Christ, p 12; Let us, p. 46: Reproduced with permission from *Augustine Day by Day* by Fr. John E. Rotelle, OSA, © 1986 Catholic Book Publishing Co., New York. All rights reserved.

With the, p. 12; You show, p. 41: *The Prayers of Catherine of Siena,* © 1993 Suzanne Noffke. Paulist Press, Mahwah, New Jersey.

Hear our, p. 14; Lord Jesus Christ, p. 20; Lord Jesus, p. 20; Lord Jesus, teach, p. 23; Blessed Lord, p. 24; A son, p. 31; Grant us, p. 38; Lord, temper, p 38; Let not, p. 40; Let us, p. 51; O Lord, p. 53: *The New Book of Christian Prayers* compiled by Tony Castle. The Crossroad Publishing Company, New York, 1986.

The adult, p. 15; Listening, p. 19: *Religious Potential of the Child,* LTP.

Please, Lamb, p. 16: *The Voyage of the Dawn Treader,* Scholastic, Inc., New York, 1952.

Listening, p. 18: *Guide for the Assembly*, LTP.

We begin, p. 25; Brothers, p. 48; In the, p. 52: Used by permission from *Toward God*, © 1989, 1995 Michael Casey; Liguori Publications, Liguori, Missouri.

Let us, p. 26: *The Violence of Love*, © Plough Publishing House, Farmington, Pennsylvania. Used by permission.

Above all, p. 28: *Revised English Bible*.

O Lord, p. 29: *Selected Prayers*, tr. Keith R. Crim. John Knox Press, Richmond, Virginia, 1965.

Dear Lord, p. 30: Composed for this publication.

My Lord, p. 32: Excerpt from "The Love of Solitude" from *Thoughts in Solitude*, © 1956, 1958, The Abbey of Our Lady of Gethsemani, renewed 1986, the Trustees of the Merton Legacy Trust. Used with permission of Paulist Press.

It helps, p. 36: *Action in Waiting* by Christopher Blumhardt, © 1998 Plough Publishing House. Used by permission.

Teach me, p. 39; Be present, p. 42; Lord, help, p. 57: *In the Presence of My Father*, tr. and comp. Laurence Brett. Helicon Press, Inc., Baltimore, Maryland, 1968.

Lord, p. 47; Somewhere, p. 59: *A Basket of Bread*, © 1972—1996, Catherine de Vinck. Alba House, Staten Island, New York.

For the, p. 49: *Praying the Bible*, tr. Edward Hagmar. The Liturgical Press, Collegeville.

Oh Book, p. 54: *Chapters into Verse: Poetry in English Inspired by the Bible, vol. 1*. Assembled and edited by Robert Atwan and Laurance Wider. Oxford University Press, New York, 1993.

How is, p. 55: *Noteworthy* published by Carmel of St. Joseph, Terre Haute, Indiana.

There is, p. 55: *An Interrupted Life: The Diaries of Etty Hillesum 1941-1943*. Translation © 1983 Jonathan Cape Ltd. Pantheon Books.

Late have, p. 56: *The Confessions*, tr. Marie Boulding, OSB, ©1997 Augustinian Heritage Institute. Used by permission.

You wait, p. 58: *Your Word Is Near*, tr. N. D. Smith. Paulist Press.